A Maggot in the Mouthwash

The Spirals Series

Plays

Jan Carew
Computer Killer

Chris Culshaw
Dribs and Drabs
Gaffs and Laughs
Radio Riff-Raff

Christine Dawe
The Wanna Beez

Julia Donaldson
Books and Crooks

Nigel Gray
An Earwig in the Ear

Angela Griffiths
TV Hospital
Wally and Co

Paul Groves
Tell Me Where it Hurts

Julia Pattison
Kicking Up a Stink

Bill Ridgway
Monkey Business

John Townsend
A Bit of a Shambles
Cheer and Groan
Chef's Night Off
Clogging the Works
Cowboys, Jelly and Custard
Gulp and Gasp
Hiccups and Slip-ups
Jumping the Gun
A Lot of Old Codswallop
A Maggot in the Mouthwash
Murder at Muckleby Manor

David Walke
The Good, the Bad and the Bungle
Package Holiday

Non-fiction

Jim Alderson
Crash in the Jungle

Jan Carew
Eyam, Plague Village

Chris Culshaw
Dive into Danger
Ground Zero

David Orme
Hackers

Jill Ridge
Lifelines

Bill Ridgway
Break Out!
Lost in Alaska
Over the Wall
A Soldiers Tale

Julie Taylor
Lucky Dip

John Townsend
Burke and Hare: The Body Snatchers
Kingdom of the Man-eaters
Raiders of the Dome Diamond
Trapped Under Ground

Keith West
Back to the Wild
The Great Trek

Fiction

Jim Alderson
The Witch Princess

Penny Bates
Tiger of the Lake

Jan Carew
Footprints in the Sand
Voices in the Dark

Susan Duberley
The Ring

John Goodwin
Ghost Train

Angela Griffiths
Diary of a Wild Thing
Stories of Suspense

Anita Jackson
The Actor
The Austin Seven
Bennet Manor
Dreams
The Ear
A Game of Life and Death
No Rent to Pay

Paul Jennings
Eye of Evil
Maggot

Richard Kemble
Grandmother's Secret

Helen Lowerson
The Biz

Margaret Loxton
The Dark Shadow

Bill Ridgway
The Hawkstone
The Last Trip to Oron
The Power of the Hawkstone
Mr Punch
Spots

John Townsend
Back on the Prowl
Beware the Morris Minor
A Minute to Kill
Night Beast
Snow Beast
Sweet Dreams

NEW Spirals *PLAYS*

A Maggot in the Mouthwash

John Townsend

Text © John Townsend 2004

The right of John Townsend to be identified as the author of this work has been asserted by him in accordance with the Copyright, Designs and Patents Act 1988.

All rights reserved. No part of this publication may be reproduced or transmitted in any form or by any means, electronic or mechanical, including photocopy, recording or any information storage and retrieval system, without permission in writing from the publisher or under licence from the Copyright Licensing Agency Limited, 90 Tottenham Court Road, London W1T 4LP.

Any person who commits any unauthorised act in relation to this publication may be liable to criminal prosecution and civil claims for damages.

Published in 2004 by:
Nelson Thornes Ltd
Delta Place
27 Bath Road
CHELTENHAM
GL53 7TH
United Kingdom

04 05 06 07 08 / 10 9 8 7 6 5 4 3 2 1

A catalogue record for this book is available from the British Library

ISBN 0-7487-9017-9

Cover illustration by Ian Jackson
Page make-up by Tech-Set, Gateshead

Printed in Croatia by Zrinski

Contents

Four dentist plays to make you shudder, each for two parts.

A Maggot in the Mouthwash ———————————————— 4

2 parts: Dentist

          Patient

Spare Parts ———————————————————————————— 16

2 parts: Dentist

          Patient

Sealed with a Kiss ———————————————————— 23

2 parts: Teacher

          Receptionist

Crossed Wires ————————————————————————— 32

2 parts: Caretaker

          Sam

A Maggot in the Mouthwash

2 parts: Dentist
          Patient (who speaks with a bit of a whistle when saying an 's')

Scene: A dentist's surgery.

Dentist   Come in.

Patient   [Rushing in] At last. I'm in agony.

Dentist   Then you'd better open wide and let me take a look.

Patient   It's not my mouth that hurts. It's that waiting room.

Dentist   Waiting room?

Patient   All those toys. I've been sitting on an Action Man and a lump of Lego for half an hour. It wasn't very nice, I can tell you.

Dentist   I don't suppose the Action Man liked it either!

Patient   I tried to see you yesterday but you weren't here.

Dentist   No. I was off sick. Take a seat.

Patient	Nothing too bad, I hope.
Dentist	I just had a spot of toothache.
Patient	A dentist with toothache? Where does a dentist go if he has toothache?
Dentist	The pub. I hope you don't mind me saying – but you sound odd.
Patient	You can say that again. I'm in a sorry state.
Dentist	Your 's' sounds strange. Like a whistle. Does it bother you?
Patient	Not as much as it bothers all the dogs up our street.
Dentist	How long have you been like this?
Patient	Since my lettuce and sausage sandwich last Sunday.
Dentist	A lettuce and sausage sandwich?
Patient	With salad cream, spicy sauce and sesame seeds.
Dentist	With salad cream, spicy sauce and sesame seeds?
Patient	You're repeating what I say.
Dentist	Sorry. I have a habit of repeating.
Patient	So did my sandwich.
Dentist	So how can I help?

Patient	Just take a look. I keep talking funny.
Dentist	Great. I like people telling jokes.
Patient	No. Not funny. Odd. My whistle.
Dentist	Well, I'd better take a look. Just lie back.
Patient	Something snapped.
Dentist	Did it? Where? I didn't hear it. Was it my chair?
Patient	No – in my mouth. It was that sandwich. Something seemed to snap.
Dentist	Was there pain?
Patient	No pain.
Dentist	Was there a tingle?
Patient	No tingle.
Dentist	Was there a crack, a sting, a wobble or a scrape?
Patient	No stings or scrapes. Just a sensation.
Dentist	A sensation?
Patient	A slither. Something seemed to slither.
Dentist	You'd better open wide.
Patient	[*Opening mouth wide*] Aaa glar urgle.
Dentist	Not your mouth – your wallet. This could be expensive. Just my joke!
Patient	Car coo kee anky kink?

Dentist I beg your pardon?

Patient Can you see anything?

Dentist I've got some good news and some bad news.

Patient What is it?

Dentist Good news – your teeth are fine. Bad news – your gums will have to come out.

Patient Are you serious?

Dentist No. It's just another joke.

Patient I thought you must be joking. You gave a wink.

Dentist Did I? Oh dear. That means my eye is on the blink. It's playing up. Open wide again.

Patient Aaaa

Dentist Oh dear.

Patient What can you see?

Dentist Nothing. My contact lens has come out. Don't move.

Patient Now you've got one eye shut.

Dentist Don't worry, I'll carry on with one eye. You open your mouth and I'll shut my eye. Okay? [*They both do so*]

Patient Argh ack ugah

Dentist	Mmm.
Patient	Oog org grugah
Dentist	Mmm.
Patient	Erg eeg krick og ow ark.
Dentist	Mmm. Probably. Have you been on your holidays yet?
Patient	Ech. Grikon.
Dentist	Lovely. We went there last year. Nice weather?
Patient	Ock koo gag.
Dentist	Jolly good. Ah ha.
Patient	Ack koo ow ung kink?
Dentist	I think so. Hold tight while I pull.
Patient	Aaaeeeeergh!
Dentist	Got it. There. Rinse out your mouth.
Patient	That was a strange sensation.
Dentist	Have you noticed something?
Patient	Yes. I can speak without sounding funny.
Dentist	Just gargle a bit with the mouthwash.
Patient	[*Gargles*] That's much better. What did you do?
Dentist	I just gave a little prod here and a squeeze there.

Patient   All with one eye shut. Very clever.

Dentist   Tell me about that lettuce and sausage sandwich.

Patient   It was very nice with salad cream, spicy sauce and sesame seeds.

Dentist   Was it sort of squidgy?

Patient   Squidgy?

Dentist   Or slippery?

Patient   Slippery?

Dentist   Or even slimy?

Patient   Slimy?

Dentist   You must like gardening.

Patient   Oh yes. Now and again.

Dentist   You like to grow a few bits and bobs?

Patient   Now and again.

Dentist   Like lettuce. You grow your own?

Patient   Now and again.

Dentist   Do you wash your lettuce?

Patient   Now and again.

Dentist   I mean scrub it.

Patient   Why do you ask?

Dentist   Take a look at my tweezers.

Patient   What is it?

Dentist   Half a slug.

Patient   That's just a bit worse than finding a whole slug.

Dentist   It was squashed between your back teeth.

Patient   That's terrible news.

Dentist   Oh don't worry. It would have died without pain.

Patient   It's gross!

Dentist   But don't worry – it didn't die alone.

Patient   I beg your pardon?

Dentist   There was this as well.

Patient   What is it?

Dentist   A big fat hairy caterpillar.

Patient   A whole one?

Dentist   I'm afraid not. Just half.

Patient   I feel sick.

Dentist   But that's not all. Do you see these?

Patient   What are they?

Dentist   Lots of little eggs. They were stuck inside your tooth cavity.

Patient   What sort of eggs?

Dentist Er . . . are you ready for this?

Patient Tell me.

Dentist Cockroach.

Patient I'm never going to eat a lettuce again.

Dentist Let me give you some advice about a filling.

Patient Not now. I couldn't face having a filling today.

Dentist No – my advice about fillings is this. Always wash it first and sprinkle it with salt. Tomato and cheese is the best.

Patient What are you talking about?

Dentist Fillings. Sandwich fillings. You just need a bit of practice.

Patient I'm never going to eat a sandwich again.

Dentist Oh, by the way . . . there was something else on your wisdom tooth.

Patient Don't tell me. I can't bear any more. Was it an earwig or half a worm? Maybe a plump bug or a juicy spider.

Dentist No – even better. Look – my contact lens! I found it in your mouth! I can see now.

Patient Lucky for you.

Dentist   Not really. It means I can now see the mouthwash.

Patient   What about it?

Dentist   When you rinsed out your mouth, you flushed out a couple of things.

Patient   Really?

Dentist   Yes. One was a bit of Lego. You must have got that from the waiting room!

Patient   What else is in the mouthwash?

Dentist   A rather plump maggot.

Patient   Oh no. Don't say it's in half and sinking to the bottom.

Dentist   Not at all. In fact it's looking very healthy and doing front crawl.

Patient   [*Running to the door*] I'm feeling ill. I've got to get out of here.

Dentist   Don't worry about it. It's all over now.

Patient   No it isn't. You might have a waiting room full in a minute.

Dentist   Why is that?

Patient   Aren't you forgetting something? I run a pub. I served hundreds of my lettuce sandwiches last week. They could all sue me. What if they all ate a maggot?

Dentist Simple. Just tell them it's what you describe on the board outside your pub.

Patient But it just says 'Pub Grub'.

Dentist Exactly. You can't beat a nice juicy pub grub with lettuce!

[*Blackout*]

Spare Parts

2 parts: Dentist
Patient (a little strange, scatty and oddly dressed)

Scene: A dentist's surgery. Patient falls into the room, dropping shopping and sending things flying.

Dentist   Come in and sit down.

Patient   Good. I'm in a bit of a hurry.

Dentist   How are things?

Patient   It's been one of those days.

Dentist   Any problems?

Patient   Yes. My drains are blocked, the cat's got fleas and I've lost my glasses.

Dentist   I see.

Patient   Well I don't. I've had to come out in the wrong glasses.

Dentist   I'm over here! Well I suppose it could be worse.

Patient   Could it?

Dentist   Yes. You could have lost the drains, got a blocked cat and your glasses could have fleas!

Patient	This is a funny coat hanger.
Dentist	You've just hung your coat on my assistant.
Patient	I must get these glasses looked at.
Dentist	Come and lie on the chair.
Patient	I'm a bit stressed.
Dentist	Relax. I'm used to people being nervous.
Patient	It's a big night for me tonight. That's why I'm here.
Dentist	Really?
Patient	[*Sitting on dentist's chair*] I want you to make me look lovely.
Dentist	Really?
Patient	For tonight. I'm meeting someone very special at The Palace.
Dentist	Really? You're meeting The Queen at Buckingham Palace?
Patient	No. It's the manager at The Palace in the High Street. Tonight is bingo night.
Dentist	Oh. Then I'd better polish things up a bit, eh?
Patient	Polish? I don't want polish. I need a trim, shampoo and set and a few tints. This is a funny chair.

Dentist   I beg your pardon?

Patient   It's a funny chair. It doesn't normally go this far back.

Dentist   I've had this chair ten years.

Patient   It said in your advert in the paper that you've got a special offer.

Dentist   Really?

Patient   Yes. £5 off with extra custard creams.

Dentist   Pardon?

Patient   Custard creams. I normally get a cup of coffee but this week it's custard creams as well. Free.

Dentist   Er . . . I think you've made a bit of a mistake.

Patient   No. I know my glasses aren't very good but I saw it in the paper. 'Coffee and custard creams free'.

Dentist   If I gave people biscuits, I'd get into a lot of trouble!

Patient   Ah, good – there's my drink . . . [*Sipping the mouthwash*] I don't think much of your coffee. It's stone cold for one thing. It tastes terrible and it looks a bit pink. I'd sack your tea-girl if I were you.

Dentist I think your glasses could do with a clean. They're covered in paint. Have you been decorating?

Patient No – I walked into the ladder outside the library.

Dentist They're painting the library.

Patient Not now they're not. The painter landed in the road.

Dentist Is that what all the noise was? I heard the ambulance arrive.

Patient So did I. They were very rude. How was I to know it was an ambulance? I stood there for five minutes asking for a choc-ice, a Magnum and a raspberry ripple.

Dentist Perhaps you should have those glasses seen to.

Patient I know. I just went into Specs-R-Us to get them changed.

Dentist Well didn't they help?

Patient No. It wasn't Specs-R-Us at all. I was in Spud-U-Like. Still, I got a very nice jacket potato with garlic and onion.

Dentist Then I'd better get a peg for my nose when you open your mouth wide.

19

Patient   Open my mouth wide? Why should I do that?

Dentist   Because I'm a dentist.

Patient   A dentist? What are you doing working as a hairdresser?

Dentist   I'm not . . .

Patient   You can't be a very good dentist if you have to do this job as well.

Dentist   This isn't the hairdresser.

Patient   Nonsense. My glasses might be bad but I saw all those brushes as I came in.

Dentist   They're toothbrushes.

Patient   That's a relief. I thought they looked rather small. I thought my glasses had got worse.

Dentist   So what shall we do about your teeth?

Patient   My teeth are fine. I want my hair cut.

Dentist   Then I'm afraid you'll have to go next door for that.

Patient   Why can't you do it? I'm sure you could make my hair look nice.

Dentist   All I can do is floss your roots, straighten the teeth of your comb and give you a crown. How's that?

Patient	That's no good. I want you to make me look stunning.
Dentist	Try the Magic Shop on the corner.
Patient	As I'm here, you may as well make my teeth look gleaming and sparkling. Can you make me look like a film star?
Dentist	How about The Incredible Hulk?
Patient	How long would it take you to make them straight and spotless?
Dentist	A few hours.
Patient	In that case, you can work on my teeth while I pop next door to get my hair done.
Dentist	How can I do that?
Patient	Simple. [*Takes out teeth and plonks them on the table*] They're false. Do something with these and I'll pop back in a jiffy.
Dentist	I'll need longer than that. Besides, you'll be most of the day at that hairdresser!
Patient	No I won't. I've got things to do. [*Standing to go*] Besides, it's only a wig. I'll drop it off and collect it later!
Dentist	Wow! It must make life so much easier when you just drop things off to get them seen to like that!

Patient   You bet. But they get a bit upset sometimes. You'll hear the screams in a minute.

Dentist   Why's that?

Patient   I'm popping into the opticians next!

[*Blackout*]

Sealed with a Kiss

2 parts: Teacher (who needs urgent help)
         Receptionist (not very helpful)

Scene: A dentist's waiting room.

Teacher	[*Rushing in looking hot, bothered and wet*] Quick!
Receptionist	Good afternoon.
Teacher	No it's not. Quick.
Receptionist	Just take a seat.
Teacher	A dentist is needed.
Receptionist	No thank you – we've already got one.
Teacher	It's an emergency.
Receptionist	Then you'll need to phone that number on this card.
Teacher	That's no good.
Receptionist	I think you'll find it suits most people.
Teacher	No – there's a problem.
Receptionist	Then take a seat and we'll sort it out in good time.
Teacher	I haven't got good time.

23

Receptionist   That's a shame.

Teacher   [*Raising voice a little*] Don't I make myself clear?

Receptionist   I think so. Please sit down.

Teacher   I don't want to sit down. There's been an accident.

Receptionist   Name?

Teacher   Sorry?

Receptionist   I'll need your surname and postcode.

Teacher   Why? This isn't my dentist.

Receptionist   Then you'll have to fill in a form. Here you are.

Teacher   It's not for me. I don't need a dentist.

Receptionist   [*Snatching the form back*] That's funny – you just said you did.

Teacher   I've run here from the park.

Receptionist   That's a long way. I hope you didn't get too wet. Terrible storm.

Teacher   That's the reason I'm here.

Receptionist   Well I'm sorry but this isn't a shelter, you know. Try next door at the launderette.

Teacher	Look, I'm here to fetch the dentist.
Receptionist	Did you say 'fetch'?
Teacher	That's right. The dentist is needed in a hurry.
Receptionist	We don't do home visits.
Teacher	We need a dentist at the park.
Receptionist	We don't do park visits either. We're very busy. So sorry we can't help. We don't see non-members, I'm afraid.
Teacher	Right. In that case I'll join. Now.
Receptionist	Here are the forms. There's pink if you want full cover. There's blue if you just want check-ups every six months. There's green if you just want a polish. There's peach if you need special treatment.
Teacher	Yes, that's it. Peach. It's very special.
Receptionist	That's £300, please.
Teacher	Fine. Will that mean the dentist can come to the park right now?
Receptionist	Sorry, I'm afraid not. Not on a Tuesday.

Teacher	Then what colour form do I need for that?
Receptionist	There isn't one.
Teacher	Well make one. Any colour you like. Just for me. I'll pay £500 up front.
Receptionist	You seem stressed.
Teacher	That's right.
Receptionist	Is there a problem?
Teacher	That's right.
Receptionist	What seems to be the matter?
Teacher	Nothing. Nothing SEEMS to be the matter. The matter is staring many people straight in the face. Right now. In the park.
Receptionist	Is it something serious?
Teacher	It's like this. The school fete is on today in the park. Right now. As we speak.
Receptionist	That's right. My son is at that school. I know what's going on. You don't have to tell me.
Teacher	So do you know the P.E. teacher?
Receptionist	Oh yes. Nice man. Lovely track suit.

Teacher	He dressed up as Mister Hulk, The Strongest Man Alive.
Receptionist	How nice.
Teacher	It's to raise funds for a new school minibus.
Receptionist	Good for him.
Teacher	And for just £5 you could get a ride in a cart . . .
Receptionist	What fun.
Teacher	Pulled by Mister Hulk – just with his teeth.
Receptionist	What a nice idea. How far is the ride?
Teacher	Along by the river.
Receptionist	What a shame it just rained.
Teacher	That's the point. That's why I'm here.
Receptionist	I don't quite follow you.
Teacher	That dreadful boy in my class spoilt it all.
Receptionist	What a shame. What did he do?
Teacher	He put Superglue on the handle of the cart.
Receptionist	That's awful. What a nasty child.

27

Teacher	So the poor P.E. teacher is not happy. His teeth are stuck rigid. They won't budge. They're stuck on the handle of the cart.
Receptionist	What a shame. I bet he told that boy off.
Teacher	He can't speak. He just grunts.
Receptionist	That's P.E. teachers for you.
Teacher	He was pulling the cart along by the river when a flash of lightning struck the cart.
Receptionist	How nasty.
Teacher	The cart flew right off the path.
Receptionist	Fancy that.
Teacher	And the poor man is now hanging on for grim death. The cart is hanging over the river and he can't bite much longer. His gums are going.
Receptionist	Well let's face it – it was a silly thing to do. I bet he didn't do a risk assessment. At least no one is in danger.
Teacher	Yes they are. Two pupils are in the cart. They're hanging on for dear life just above the river.

Receptionist	Why don't they jump out?
Teacher	They can't. That terrible boy with the Superglue was in the cart with his girlfriend.
Receptionist	That's nice.
Teacher	They were kissing.
Receptionist	That's the young people of today for you.
Teacher	But the lightning struck and locked them together.
Receptionist	Locked them together?
Teacher	The braces on their teeth fused. His fused to hers.
Receptionist	Fused?
Teacher	Melted. Welded. They're joined to each other at the mouth and can't move.
Receptionist	If you ask me it serves the little beggar right.
Teacher	But with the storm and heavy rain, the river is rising fast. If the dentist doesn't hurry up with his drill and hacksaw to cut them free, they'll all drown.

29

Receptionist Oh dear.

Teacher [*Now shouting*] SO WHAT ARE YOU GOING TO DO ABOUT IT?

Receptionist There's no need to shout. It's more than my job is worth to disturb the dentist right now.

Teacher But there's a crisis. Pupils may DIE!

Receptionist You can't blame me for that. Blame the parents of that ghastly child in your class. They should have brought him up properly.

Teacher [*Finally snapping*] All right, that's it! I've tried. I've tried to tell you as best I could. Now watch my lips. THAT BRAT OF A SON OF YOURS IS STUCK TO A GIRL'S MOUTH IN THE BACK OF A CART. THEY'RE HANGING OVER A RAGING RIVER WITH THE P.E. TEACHER HOLDING THEM WITH HIS TEETH . . . WHICH ARE STARTING TO CRACK! There. Have you got it now?

Receptionist MY son?

Teacher That's right.

Receptionist Well why didn't you say? In that case . . .. [*Talks into the intercom on the desk*] Mr Hopkins . . .. Get out here quick. Get your drill NOW! Get down to that park and get a move on. My son's got a problem with his teeth . . .. Bless him.

[*Blackout*]

Crossed Wires

2 parts: Caretaker (in a white overall)
Sam (a stroppy teenager visiting the dentist)

Scene: An empty room next to the dentist's surgery. The Caretaker is painting the bare room. There's a chair in the middle. Sam thinks the Caretaker is the new dentist. The Caretaker thinks Sam is the new work experience student.

Caretaker	[*With a tool bag at a bench – mending a plug*] Ah, so that's the problem. Crossed wires.
Sam	[*Strolling in through the open door, with walkman on*] I'm here.
Caretaker	Ah, about time too. You're late.
Sam	Eh?
Caretaker	I wrote the time you should be here on the form.
Sam	What?
Caretaker	If you switched off that walkman you'd hear me.
Sam	Eh? Is this chair all you've got? I don't think much of this place. [*Sits on chair*] It's rubbish. It's real pants.

Caretaker	Listen, you're not here to sit down. You'll have to wait a minute while I finish this plug. The last thing you want is crossed wires.
Sam	I hate dentists.
Caretaker	Your paint and brush are over there but you can watch me first. See how it's done.
Sam	Eh?
Caretaker	Then you'll need to get some putty to fill the cracks.
Sam	What did you say?
Caretaker	Switch that thing off! If you listened, you might know what's going on.
Sam	Whatever. I hate this place. I wasn't going to come at all. I don't see the point.
Caretaker	You don't see the point? I'll soon make you see the point. You'll also see the paint.
Sam	Whatever.
Caretaker	I don't think much of your attitude.
Sam	Whatever.

Caretaker	When I was your age I'd have been over the moon to watch and learn. You're here to taste the world of work.
Sam	Whatever. I hope it tastes better than mouthwash.
Caretaker	You youngsters today expect everything handed to you on a plate.
Sam	Cool. Cheers. Are you handing out biscuits?
Caretaker	Don't be so cheeky.
Sam	Biscuits are wicked. Last time I came here I got a lecture on biscuits – and how to use a brush.
Caretaker	I'll show you how to use a brush all right. And a roller.
Sam	Whatever.
Caretaker	You'll need to keep your eyes fixed on that wall there.
Sam	Last time I had to look up at the ceiling all the time. Can't you put a picture up there like before?
Caretaker	I don't do pictures and fittings. I just do the fabric.
Sam	Whatever. This place sucks.
Caretaker	Your tin of paint is in the corner.

Sam You what?

Caretaker Open it up.

Sam Eh?

Caretaker OPEN IT!

Sam Oh, right. [*Puts head back and opens mouth wide*]

Caretaker This plug is in a right mess. I've lost my best screwdriver. I need it a lot in this job . . .. [*Sees Sam*] Are you going to sit like that all day?

Sam [*Mouth wide open*] Aaaah.

Caretaker It looks like you're catching flies. There's work to be done.

Sam I know. I'm waiting for you to get started.

Caretaker We'll have to sand things down a bit first. It looks a bit rough from here.

Sam But I cleaned them last night.

Caretaker And there are lots of cracks in the corners. We'll need a whole tub of putty to fill that lot.

Sam [*Touching teeth*] They can't be that bad! No one told me last time I need fillings and stuff.

Caretaker	You must always expect a few cracks at this stage.
Sam	Is it decay and stuff?
Caretaker	Worse.
Sam	Worse?
Caretaker	I reckon it's rising damp.
Sam	It can't be!
Caretaker	Or even dry rot.
Sam	Will it hurt?
Caretaker	You can get some good stuff now. It smells awful and you must leave it on for two weeks. You have to be careful with it as it can catch fire and give off dangerous fumes.
Sam	I don't want anything like that!
Caretaker	Don't worry. I'll try plaster first and a dab of paint.
Sam	Paint? What sort of paint?
Caretaker	Orange. It's all the rage round here. Can you give that brush a wipe?
Sam	A toothbrush?
Caretaker	Don't talk daft. You'll need a large one. 12cm wide.

Sam	I won't get that in my mouth!
Caretaker	I might get you to do the drilling, too.
Sam	Drilling? Me? How can I do it?
Caretaker	Simple. I've nearly fixed the plug. You just hold the drill with one hand, switch on and push. There's nothing to it.
Sam	There's no way I can do that!
Caretaker	It's dead easy. It's a Black and Decker power drill. Just the job. It's like cutting through butter.
Sam	I feel sick.
Caretaker	I'll need to fix a small bracket somewhere in the middle.
Sam	A bracket? What for?
Caretaker	A smoke alarm.
Sam	A smoke alarm? Whatever for?
Caretaker	We fit them all the time now. Everyone has them.
Sam	You haven't.
Caretaker	Yes I have. I've got three. I can't smoke now. Every time I light up, they go off.

Sam   Well I don't want one.

Caretaker   Some people stick them in the roof so you can't see them.

Sam   The roof of their mouth? It must make them talk funny. I'd rather have my fillings pulled out with pliers. Or have all my root canals dug out with a rusty drill – than have a smoke alarm fitted in my mouth.

Caretaker   What are you going on about? [*Looking up at the wall*] Ooh, I've just seen that nail.

Sam   [*Looking down at a red shiny thumb nail*] What's wrong with it?

Caretaker   It looks terrible.

Sam   I think it looks cool.

Caretaker   No – it will have to come out.

Sam   You what?

Caretaker   We can't leave it like that. You can do it yourself if you like.

Sam   No way!

Caretaker   Well it's got to come out. One quick pull with my pliers and you won't know it was there.

Sam   But it will hurt.

Caretaker	One sharp tug is all it will take. Here you are. It has to be done. [*Handing Sam the pliers*]
Sam	You've got to be joking.
Caretaker	No. Now stop being a wimp and get on with it. I want to test this plug I've fixed. Grip that nail with the pliers and pull. You may have to stand on the chair.
Sam	[*Standing on the chair and putting the pliers slowly on the thumb nail*] But I don't want to . . ..
Caretaker	[*Switching on the plug – there is a bang and Sam screams, falls off the chair and pulls out the nail!*] That's the problem when you get your wires crossed!
Sam	[*Waving the pliers and having a tantrum*] Now look what you've made me do! I never wanted to come here anyway. I'm not letting you paint my teeth orange. You're not going to fill them with putty and stuff. You're never going to fit a smoke alarm in my mouth. Never! I HATE YOU! [*Runs out*]
Caretaker	[*Looking puzzled for a few seconds*] Whatever! [*Blackout*]

If you enjoyed this play, why not try these other NEW SPIRALS medical plays:

An Earwig in the Ear by Nigel Gray
Tell Me Where It Hurts by Paul Groves
TV Hospital by Angela Griffiths